EDLE toot stumble ZOOMB. rap ping TAP
atter HOWL tap flap flap YO SCU
SWISH BOO splatter drip rattle
LOW PING wiggle tingle TUMBLE TAP SLOSH BONG deed-a BOO SLAP ziggildy click
SH plop tap WHISTLE ROAR click clickety-clack BOO swish
ping SLISH bong TAP TAP SPLASH SPLISH TAP TA
RUMBLE clang drop squiggle dunder clap dri
shag ping PUMP-A-RUM SLOSH A GALOSH CLAN
H-PA-RAH flip flop slurp THUNDER plop BANG BASH clap cla
HOOT slip slap clang WIGGLE PING SLITHER BONG flop
vl blunder tootle-too flip stumble bang clatter BOO tingle rat
LE clunk QUIVER slurp flap TOOT HOOT clap clunk
YOWL rap tap tap CRASH SWASH slip slap plip
kety-clack SCATTER slosh CLANG swish slosh rattle batter TH
osh clang clap drip drop TAP SWISH BASH whis
YOWL THUMP bber oo whistle TOOT IGGLE SLU pumBONG
swish HOOT Q

for Michael Smith

## OXFORD
### UNIVERSITY PRESS

Great Clarendon Street, Oxford OX2 6DP

Oxford University Press is a department of the University of Oxford.
It furthers the University's aim of excellence in research, scholarship,
and education by publishing worldwide in

Oxford New York

Auckland Bangkok Buenos Aires Cape Town Chennai
Dar es Salaam Delhi Hong Kong Istanbul Karachi Kolkata
Kuala Lumpur Madrid Melbourne Mexico City Mumbai Nairobi
São Paulo Shanghai Taipei Tokyo Toronto

Oxford is a registered trade mark of Oxford University Press
in the UK and in certain other countries

First published 1987
Reprinted 1988, 1989 (twice), 1990, 1992, 1993

First published in paperback 1989

ISBN 0–19–278219–3 (Paperback)

20 19 18

The editor and publisher are grateful for permission to reprint the following copyright poems.

Elizabeth Coatsworth: 'Rhyme'. Copyright © 1960 Elizabeth Coatsworth. Eleanor Farjeon: 'J is for Jazz-Man' from *Silver Sand and
Snow* (Michael Joseph). Reprinted by permission of David Higham Associates Limited. Jimmy Garthwaite: 'Engineers'from Puddin'
An' Pie, copyright 1929 by HarperCollins Publishers, Renewed 1957 by Mirle Garthwaite. Reprinted by permission of HarperCollins
Publishers, Dahlov Ipcar: 'Fishes Evening Song' from *Whisperings and Other Things* (Alfred A Knopf, 1967), copyright © 1967 by
Dahlov Ipcar. Reprinted by permission of McIntosh and Otis, Inc, David McCord: 'Song of the Train' from *One At A Time*, copyright
1952 by David McCord. Reprinted by permission of Little, Brown and Company. Eve Merriam: 'Weather' from *Catch a Little Rhyme*,
copyright © 1966 by Eve Merriam, © renewed 1994 Dee Michel and Guy Michel. Reprinted by permission of Marian Reiner. Spike
Milligan: 'On the Ning Nang Nong' from *Silly Verse For Kids and Animals* (Michael Joseph Ltd.). Reprinted by permission of Spike
Milligan Productions Ltd. Tao Lang Pee: 'Sampan', published in Wheel Around the World (ed. Chris Searle, Macdonald & Co.). Jack
Prelutsky: 'Spaghetti! Spaghetti!' from *Rainy Day Saturday*, copyright © 1980 by Jack Prelutsky; 'The Yak' from *Zoo Doings*, copyright
© 1967, 1983 by Jack Prelutsky. Both reprinted by permission of Greenwillow Books (A Division of William Morrow & Company Inc.).
Barbara Ireson: 'The Small Ghostie' from Rhyme Time (Hamlyn), copyright Barbara Ireson. Reprinted by permission of the author.
James Reeves: 'The Ceremonial Band' from *Complete Poems for Children* (Heinemann), © James Reeves Estate. Reprinted by
permission of the James Reeves Estate.

Although every effort has been made to obtain copyright permission this has not proved possible in every instance. If notified the
publisher will be pleased to rectify any omissions at the earliest opportunity.

Typeset by Oxford Publishing Services

Printed in China

# NOISY
# POEMS

COLLECTED BY JILL BENNETT

ILLUSTRATED BY NICK SHARRATT

OXFORD UNIVERSITY PRESS

# THE CEREMONIAL BAND

(To be said out loud by a chorus and solo voices)

The old King of Dorchester,
He had a little orchestra,
And never did you hear such a
                    ceremonial band.
  'Tootle-too,' said the flute,
  'Deed-a-reedle,' said the fiddle,
For the fiddles and the flutes were
                    the finest in the land.

The old King of Dorchester,
He had a little orchestra,
And never did you hear such a
                    ceremonial band.
  'Pump-a-rum,' said the drum,
  'Tootle-too,' said the flute,
  'Deed-a-reedle,' said the fiddle,
For the fiddles and the flutes were
                    the finest in the land.

The old King of Dorchester,
He had a little orchestra,
And never did you hear such a
                    ceremonial band.
  'Pickle-pee,' said the fife,
  'Pump-a-rum,' said the drum,
  'Tootle-too,' said the flute,
  'Deed-a-reedle,' said the fiddle,
For the fiddles and the flutes were
                    the finest in the land.

The old King of Dorchester,
He had a little orchestra,
And never did you hear such a
                    ceremonial band.
  'Zoomba-zoom,' said the bass,
  'Pickle-pee,' said the fife,
  'Pump-a-rum,' said the drum,
  'Tootle-too,' said the flute,
  'Deed-a-reedle,' said the fiddle,
For the fiddles and the flutes were
                    the finest in the land.

The old King of Dorchester,
He had a little orchestra,
And never did you hear such a
                    ceremonial band.
  'Pah-pa-rah,' said the trumpet,
  'Zoomba-zoom,' said the bass,
  'Pickle-pee,' said the fife,
  'Pump-a-rum,' said the drum,
  'Tootle-too,' said the flute,
  'Deed-a-reedle,' said the fiddle,
For the fiddles and the flutes were
                    the finest in the land,
Oh! the fiddles and the flutes were
                    the finest in the land!

James Reeves

# ON THE NING NANG NONG

On the Ning Nang Nong
Where the Cows go Bong!
And the Monkeys all say Boo!
There's a Nong Nang Ning
Where the trees go Ping!
And the tea pots Jibber Jabber Joo.
On the Nong Ning Nang
All the mice go Clang!
And you can't catch 'em when they do!
So it's Ning Nang Nong!
Cows go Bong!
Nong Nang Ning!
Trees go Ping!
Nong Ning Nang!
The mice go Clang!
What a noisy place to belong,
Is the Ning Nang Ning Nang Nong!

Spike Milligan

## SONG OF THE TRAIN

Clickety-clack,
Wheels on the track,
This is the way
They begin the attack:
Click-ety-clack,
Click-ety-clack,
Click-ety, *clack-ety,*
Click-ety
Clack.

Clickety-clack,
Over the crack,
Faster and faster
The song of the track:
Clickety-clack,
Clickety-clack,
Clickety, clackety,
*Clackety*
Clack.

Riding in front,
Riding in back,
*Everyone* hears
The song of the track:
Clickety-clack
Clickety-clack,
Clickety-*clickety*
Clackety
*Clack.*

David McCord

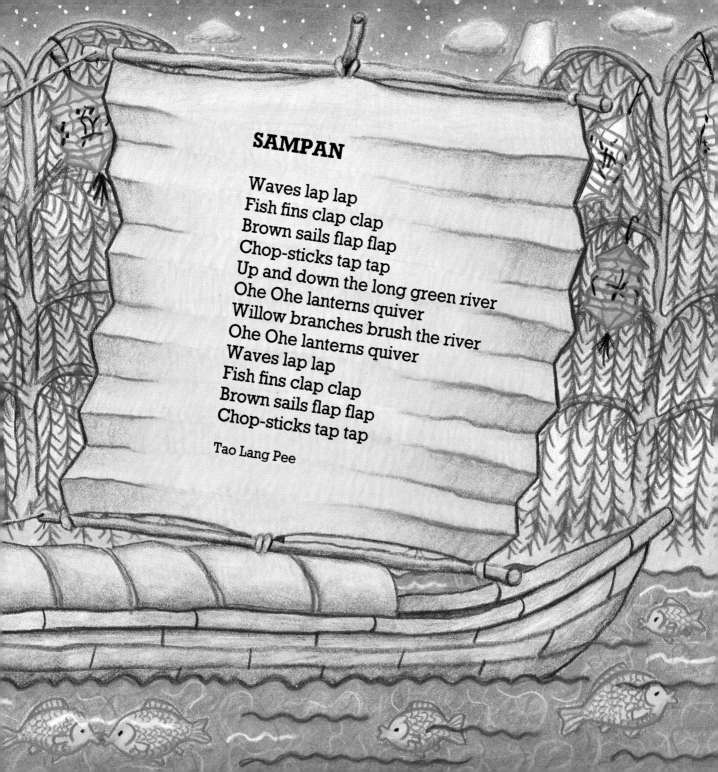

# SAMPAN

Waves lap lap
Fish fins clap clap
Brown sails flap flap
Chop-sticks tap tap
Up and down the long green river
Ohe Ohe lanterns quiver
Willow branches brush the river
Ohe Ohe lanterns quiver
Waves lap lap
Fish fins clap clap
Brown sails flap flap
Chop-sticks tap tap

Tao Lang Pee

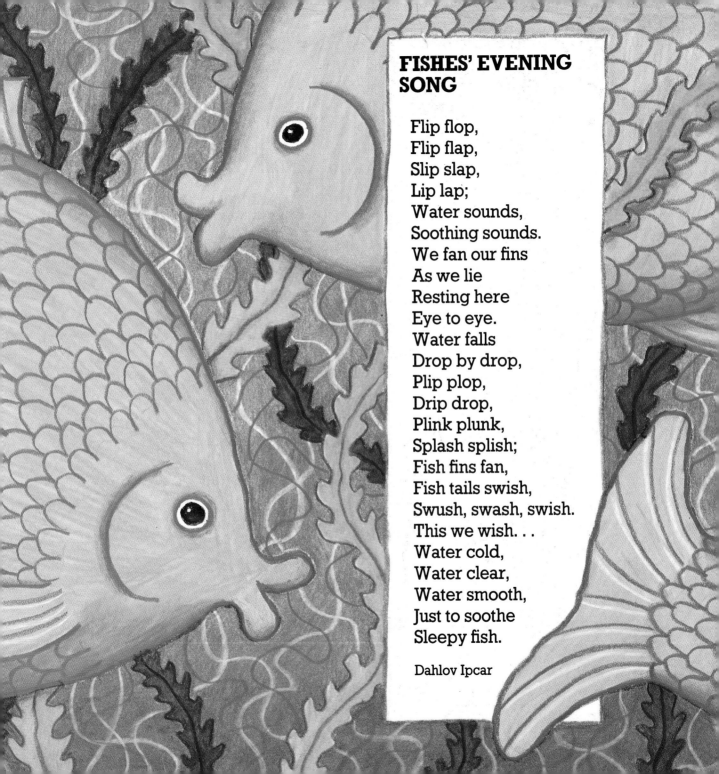

# FISHES' EVENING SONG

Flip flop,
Flip flap,
Slip slap,
Lip lap;
Water sounds,
Soothing sounds.
We fan our fins
As we lie
Resting here
Eye to eye.
Water falls
Drop by drop,
Plip plop,
Drip drop,
Plink plunk,
Splash splish;
Fish fins fan,
Fish tails swish,
Swush, swash, swish.
This we wish. . .
Water cold,
Water clear,
Water smooth,
Just to soothe
Sleepy fish.

Dahlov Ipcar

# SPAGHETTI! SPAGHETTI!

Spaghetti! spaghetti!
you're wonderful stuff,
I love you, spaghetti,
I can't get enough.
You're covered with sauce
and you're sprinkled with cheese,
spaghetti! spaghetti!
oh, give me some more please.

Spaghetti! spaghetti!
piled high in a mound,
you wiggle, you wriggle,
you squiggle around.
There's slurpy spaghetti
all over my plate,
spaghetti! spaghetti!
I think you are great.

Spaghetti! spaghetti!
I love you a lot,
you're slishy, you're sloshy,
delicious and hot.
I gobble you down
oh, I can't get enough,
spaghetti! spaghetti!
you're wonderful stuff.

Jack Prelutsky

## RHYME

I like to see a thunder storm,
    A dunder storm,
        A blunder storm,
I like to see it, black and slow
Come stumbling down the hills.

I like to hear a thunder storm,
    A plunder storm,
        A wonder storm,
Roar loudly at our little house
And shake the window sills!

Elizabeth Coatsworth

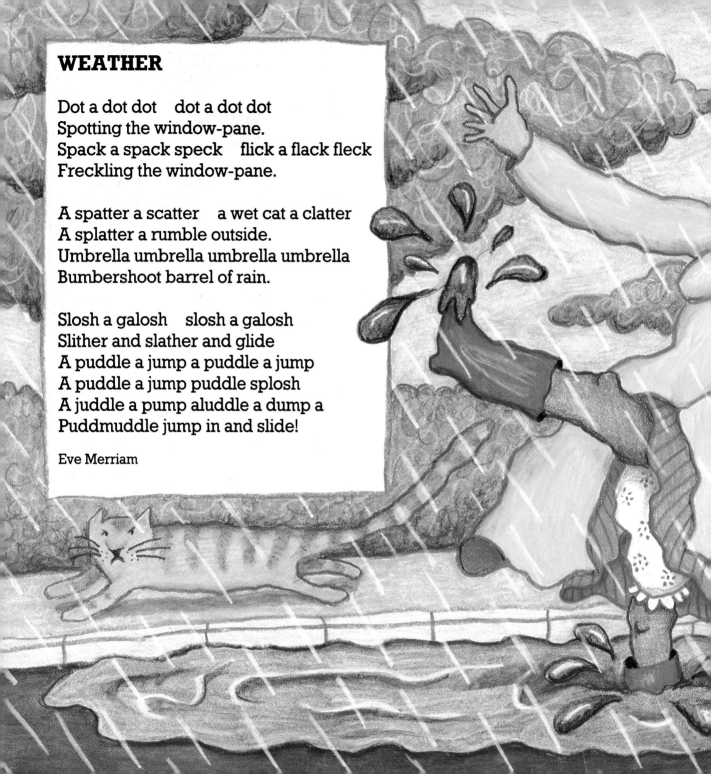

# WEATHER

Dot a dot dot   dot a dot dot
Spotting the window-pane.
Spack a spack speck   flick a flack fleck
Freckling the window-pane.

A spatter a scatter   a wet cat a clatter
A splatter a rumble outside.
Umbrella umbrella umbrella umbrella
Bumbershoot barrel of rain.

Slosh a galosh   slosh a galosh
Slither and slather and glide
A puddle a jump a puddle a jump
A puddle a jump puddle splosh
A juddle a pump aluddle a dump a
Puddmuddle jump in and slide!

Eve Merriam

## JAZZ-MAN

*Crash* and
        CLANG!
*Bash* and
        BANG!

And up in the road the Jazz-Man sprang!
The One-Man-Jazz-Band playing in the street,
Drums with his Elbows, Cymbals with his Feet,
Pipes with his Mouth, Accordion with his Hand,
Playing all his Instruments to Beat the Band!

TOOT and
        *Tingle!*
HOOT and
        *Jingle!*

Oh, what a Clatter! How the tunes all mingle!
Twenty Children couldn't make as much Noise *as*
The Howling Pandemonium of the One-Man-Jazz!

Eleanor Farjeon

## ENGINEERS

Pistons, valves and wheels and gears
That's the life of engineers
Thumping, chunking engines going
Hissing steam and whistles blowing.

There's not a place I'd rather be
Than working round machinery
Listening to that clanking sound
Watching all the wheels go round.

Jimmy Garthwaite

# THE YAK

Yickity-yackity, yickity-yak,
the yak has a scriffily, scraffily back;
some yaks are brown yaks and some yaks are black,
yickity-yackity, yickity-yak.

Sniggildy-snaggildy, sniggildy-snag,
the yak is all covered with shiggildy-shag;
he walks with a ziggildy-zaggildy-zag,
sniggildy-snaggildy, sniggildy-snag.

Yickity-yackity, yickity-yak,
the yak has a scriffily, scraffily back;
some yaks are brown yaks and some yaks are black,
yickity-yackity, yickity-yak.

Jack Prelutsky

## THE SMALL GHOSTIE

When it's late and it's dark
And everyone sleeps. . . shhh shhh shhh,
Into our kitchen
A small ghostie creeps. . . shhh shhh shhh.

We hear knocking and raps
And then rattles and taps,

Then he clatters and clangs
And he batters and bangs,

And he whistles and yowls
And he screeches and howls. . .

So we pull up our covers over our heads
And we block up our ears and WE STAY IN OUR BEDS

Barbara Ireson

ickety HISS IGGLE too HOO plip p BLED-

plop

rap SPLASH jingle hoot TAP knock flap HOO plip p sniggildy slish slo

ping slosh TOOTLE-TOO click knock BANG BATTER plop clunk clack toot cla PLINK PLUN

ping clap Boo YICKITY-yak SLIP SLAP rap BOO plo

BONG zoomba-zoom Toot thump RATTLE slosh a galos

lurp flip clap SLITHER-yak Boo BONG clang chop du

KNOCK flap GOBBLE shake JIBBER THUNDER chop

BANG clang plop SLURP BO

SCREECH BONG pump-a-rum plip plop JABBER ping shig

TOOT ping lap lap thump ping TAP

FLICK BASH JINGLE spatter CLANK Boo pickle-pee crac

ingle plop BONG CLANG

HISS A FLACK clunk slosh Toot sniggildy-snag HOWL rap bong SQU

splish splash BANG slish CRASH slop FLIP FLOP clap tootle-too his

SWASH HOOT thunder SQUIGGLE HOOT CRASH clunk BON

SNIGGILDY slurp CLICKETY-CLACK YICKITY YAK FLIP FLOP tap clunk SCREE

slosh scatter plip plop howl

TAP ba CKITY YAK ATHER

EDLE toot stumble zoomb rap ping TAP flap FLAP YO rattle slurp Jibber Ja HOWL

atter HOWL tap flap drip SLAP

SWISH boo splatter TUMBLE TAP SLOSH BONG deed-a-ree boo swish ziggildy click

LOW PING wiggle tingle click clickety-clack BOO SPLASH SPLISH TAP TA

H plop tap WHISTLE ROAR click SLISH bong TAP TAP squiggle dunder clap dri

WHISTLE ping RUMBLE clang drop BANG BASH CLAN

shag ping PUMP-A-RUM SLOSH A GALOSH clap cla

-PA-RAH flip flop Slurp THUNDER TSLITHER plop BONG boo tingle

HOOT slip slap clang WIGGLE PING stumble bang clatter rat

blunder tootle-too slurp flap TOOT HOOT PICKLE-PE clap

LE clunk QUIVER rap tap tap CRASH HOOT clunk

OWL kety-clack Scatter drip drop CLANG SWASH slip slap plip

ong slosh SWISH slosh rattle batter TH

osh clang clap THUMP bber joo LA whistle TOOT IGGLE BASH whis

YOWL swish boo R HOOT SLU pump BONG Q